Active Every

kS1

Active Every Day
kS1

10-minute activities
for a healthy school day

Linda Kelly • *Wendy Seward*

A & C Black • London

Published in 2006 by A & C Black Publishers Ltd
36 Soho Square, London W1D 3QY
www.acblack.com

Copyright © 2006 Linda Kelly and Wendy Seward

Reprinted 2009 & 2010

ISBN : 978 0 7136 7727 0

A CIP record for this book is available from the British Library.

Note: While every effort has been made to ensure that the content of this
book is as technically accurate and as sound as possible, neither the author nor
the publisher can accept responsibility for any injury or loss sustained as a result
of the use of this material.

A & C Black uses paper produced with elemental chlorine-free pulp,
harvested from managed sustainable forests.

Acknowledgements
Cover illustration by Sheilagh Noble
Textual illustrations by Celia Hart
Cover and inside design by Fiona Grant

Typeset by Palimpsest Book Production Ltd, Grangemouth, Stirlingshire
Printed and bound in Great Britain by Caligraving Ltd, Thetford

Contents

Introduction

Why is physical activity important?

The importance of physical activity, and its links to improved levels of attainment, is nothing new. In fact, the notion of 'a healthy mind and a healthy body' is firmly embedded in history. The emphasis placed by the Government on the value of exercise and its links to the health and welfare of the nation are well documented, not only in terms of the obvious physical benefits but also in relation to citizenship and PHSE (Personal, Health and Social Education). Indeed, there are many benefits to be gained by children engaging in regular physical activity. These include:

- essential health benefits – developing an efficient, healthy heart and building strong muscles and bones;

- the reduction of body fat – exercise coupled with a sensible diet can vastly reduce the rate of obesity, which is rising in the UK;

- mental health benefits – physical activity can reduce stress and anxiety;

- the development of a healthy lifestyle;

- continued involvement in physical activity and sport;

- making children feel good about themselves;

- the improvement of children's social skills;

- enhanced concentration and focus.

The National Healthy Schools Programme views regular physical activity for all pupils as an essential component of becoming a healthy school. The first of their aims is that the National Healthy Schools Programme will 'support children and young people in developing healthy behaviours'. It then explains that in order to become a healthy school certain procedures must be put into place, so that 'pupils are provided with a range of opportunities to be physically active. They understand how physical activity can help them to be more healthy, and how physical activity can improve and be part of their everyday life'.

The Government's vision for children's services, 'Every Child Matters', has five key outcomes. Two of these are 'Be Healthy' and 'Enjoy and Achieve'; like the National Healthy

Schools Programme, this provides a vision of all young people being involved in regular physical activity, having a healthy lifestyle, achieving personal and social development and enjoying recreation.

Therefore, daily physical activity should, and could quite easily, be built into every school day and every child's learning.

Why every day?

It would be difficult to think of anyone who would not agree that regular exercise is important, but why should children take part in physical activity *every day*?

- Exercise is habit forming, so needs to be undertaken regularly.

- Regular repetition of an activity leads to improvement.

- Health benefits will be observed if exercise is undertaken every day.

- To stimulate mind and body.

- To provide a balance between activity and inactivity during the day.

Recommended levels of activity

The long-term ambition of the Department for Education & Skills (DfES) and the Department for Culture, Media & Sport (DCMS) is that by 2010 children will be able to participate in at least four hours of sport each week. This will be made up of:

- at least two hours of high-quality PE and sport at school, with the expectation that this will be delivered totally within the curriculum;

- an additional 2–3 hours beyond the school day, delivered by a range of school, community and club providers (DfES and DCMS, 2003).

The government hopes that 85 per cent of all pupils aged between 5 and 16 will have achieved the minimum of two hours of high-quality PE and school sport in and out of the curriculum by 2008. The Review Group on Physical Education in Scotland (2004) also states that 'all schools and education authorities should be working towards meeting the recommendations of the Physical Activity Strategy and the Sport 21 Strategy of providing two hours' quality physical education for each child every week'. It is anticipated that this would be the minimum provision that schools would offer, since it is less than the time recommended by the British Heart Foundation, who state that for improved health 'children and young people should aim to participate in activity of at least moderate intensity for one hour every day'. The Department of Health document *Choosing Health? Choosing Activity* (2004) also concurs that 'children and young people should achieve a total of at least 60 minutes of at least moderate physical activity each day'.

This can be seen as a reaction to the rising levels of obesity in the young. According to *Choosing Health? Choosing Activity*, 16 per cent of 2–15-year-olds are now obese, which brings increased risk of health problems such as hypertension, heart disease and type 2 diabetes. The study states that we need an education system that promotes and enables physical activity. This means ensuring that children are taught in active play and that PE and activity are an integral part of every day.

Choosing Health? Choosing Activity also recommends that activity sessions in schools can be achieved very satisfactorily through several short bouts of activity of 10 minutes or more, which is the philosophy behind *Active Every Day*. We are not suggesting that *Active Every Day* should replace the two hours of physical education to which all pupils are entitled; rather, it should be seen as additional and used during the day where it will be of most benefit.

Why do the *Active Every Day* programme?

Only a few schools have developed a dedicated programme of daily physical activity, despite the fact that research has shown that the brain requires certain conditions to be able to operate to its optimum capacity (Scheuer and Mitchell, 2003). These conditions include a good supply of oxygen and the release of certain chemicals – two things that happen when we take part in physical exercise. So, a small investment of 10 minutes a day of physical activity can pay huge dividends in the classroom, with children being more focused and more willing to learn. In the long term, this could potentially play an instrumental part in improving levels of attainment and enabling each child to reach his or her full potential.

Also, if children are given a positive experience of physical activity at school, this will lay the foundations for a lifetime's involvement in regular exercise. Routines established at a young age tend to be ingrained for life, so a firm commitment to 10-minute bursts of activity, as and when required, coupled with an effective and progressive PE curriculum, should go some way to instilling in children the routine and advantages of daily activity. What better habit to develop than an improved understanding of how the body works and an enhanced opportunity to develop a healthy lifestyle?

It is clear from the research carried out into the links between physical activity and health, and the high profile that physical activity now demands on the political agenda, that this is a very real issue requiring immediate attention. *Active Every Day* does not claim to provide a 'magic bullet' that will cure all of society's ills; however, it does go some way towards improving and increasing the time given to exercise and its undeniable benefits to the nation's young people.

How to use the programme

The *Active Every Day* programme is a collection of 10-minute activities that teachers can fit in at any time during the school day, wherever and whenever it is felt to be convenient or necessary. The activities can also be formally timetabled if preferred; however, experience has found that they are better suited to being used as a response to children's (and teachers') immediate needs and should therefore be dictated by those who will most benefit from them. For example, children might have just undertaken a particularly difficult numeracy lesson and need 10 minutes of physical activity to recharge their batteries and energise their brains ready for the next lesson, and a particularly tricky concept may become less daunting if it is preceded by a short burst of adrenaline before embarking on the independent element of the task.

Some of the activities have been specially designed to be carried out in the classroom with the minimum of equipment or disruption; these would be ideal precursors to independent or group activities. Others need a larger space such as a hall or playground and may need a small amount of equipment, although the preparation time required is negligible – an important concern in a teacher's already stretched timetable!

Many of the activities have ideas for extension and simplification to suit the children with whom you are working. However, as with any resource, they may need to be adapted further to suit individuals within your class.

Music could be added to activities if desired. This could be used to change the possible pace of the session, making it more active or slowing down at the end of the activity.

All of the activities are devised to be fun, enjoyable and inclusive, as well as having the obvious physical and social benefits that accompany interactive physical participation. Children who enjoy an activity are more likely to remember it, and will often replicate it with friends in the playground or outside of school, thus increasing the potential for activity as opposed to inactivity. It should not be forgotten that fun and enjoyment are integral to children's learning and development.

The programme is divided into six main sections for ease of use and can be delivered in any order and at any time. There is also an additional section concentrating on warm-ups, cool-downs, stretching and mobility. This section includes a selection of stretching and mobilising activities that can be performed in addition to the main activity. It also contains some simple ideas for warming up and cooling down, focusing on the important principles of both. There is also an appendix, which includes some photocopiable material that can be used by the teacher if desired. These include:

- a daily physical activity record sheet for pupils, which could be used at the start and end of each term or year to show progression;

- a weekly physical activity diary for pupils, which could be used at any time to examine patterns or amounts of activity;

- a physical activity attitude questionnaire for pupils, to inform the teacher's planning;

- an activity checklist for the teacher to keep a record of which activities have been undertaken and which ones were successful.

Each of the six sections gives teachers a range of age-related ideas that they can undertake with their class. The sections are as follows:

1. Limited space activities

These activities can be performed quite easily in the classroom with a minimum of disruption. Many of them require little or no movement of furniture – only that children stand in a space behind their desks – and most require no resources. The focus is on improving children's ability to listen carefully to instructions and complete a particular task or set of tasks.

2. Control, coordination and accuracy

These activities focus on the use of basic body control, coordination and accuracy in order to perform a selection of tasks, using a variety of basic sporting equipment including balls, rackets, bean bags and targets – all equipment that should be readily available in most schools.

3. Teamwork and cooperation

These activities involve the children working as a team or a group to complete a task. Participants are required to unite as a group and show consideration for the rest of the team. This section complements much of the work being done in the PHSE curriculum and can be easily linked to circle times.

4. Stamina, speed and agility

This group of activities gives pupils the chance to experience how their breathing changes with different types of exercise. It also examines the differences between speed and stamina and looks to increase agility and awareness. These activities represent an ideal opportunity for cross-curricular links to the science and physical education programmes of study.

5. Action rhymes

This collection of traditional action rhymes is excellent for developing coordination and improving children's ability to follow a sequence of instructions. They can be adapted to suit the individual or group of children as required. Most of these can be done in the classroom with a minimum of disruption, planning or preparation.

6. Skipping activities

These activities involve limited equipment, but can have a huge impact on children's development and coordination. A range of schools across the country have publicly advocated the benefits of skipping and have rolled out the idea to include promoting positive play in the playground, even developing skipping clubs and demonstration teams. An element of care should be taken with skipping exercises as they can be strenuous and are deemed to be relatively high-impact activities. Rest time should always be built into the 10 minutes allocated. As this book is for KS1, the skipping activities are instructional and progressive. This enables children to learn the basics of skipping, to which a variety of skipping rhymes can then be added.

Timetabling issues

The advantage of the *Active Every Day* programme is its simplicity and flexibility. It can be implemented very easily in to the school timetable: there is no prescribed time in the day when the 10 minutes of activity should be carried out, so the teacher can use his or her discretion to implement a session when his or her class would benefit the most. The ideas in the programme require no additional resources other than those usually found in a primary school, therefore demanding no additional budgetary requirements. The activities can be undertaken in a variety of settings including the classroom, school hall, corridor or playground.

There is usually little point in introducing a session immediately before break or lunchtime, or immediately after. However, a wet day, when the children have been restricted to the school building over lunchtime, could prove an ideal time to focus on a controlled burst of activity to reactivate the brain ready for learning to take place.

The idea behind *Active Every Day* is to re-energise the children so they will be ready to focus on the next part of their learning. As a result, it is important that the children are allowed to cool down to an acceptable level to continue with their education. It is important that the teacher selects an appropriate activity to achieve this.

Active Every Day could easily be used to complement a school's existing system of rewards; however, withdrawal of the 10 minutes is not recommended as a punishment as this would negate the whole philosophy of the belief that exercise is an intrinsic part of everyday life.

Developing a whole-school approach to physical activity

Schools are increasingly committed to creating a healthy school environment. One of the aims of this is to try to stem the worryingly high numbers of overweight and obese children. In order to achieve success in this area, there needs to be a whole-school approach to the promotion of physical activity and a commitment to healthy living. This is often highlighted in whole-school policies, particularly in relation to the 'Every Child Matters' agenda and the relevant links to the National Healthy Schools Standard.

To increase levels of physical activity, a school needs enthusiastically to promote and enable regular participation in a variety of key areas. These could include:

- a broad and balanced high-quality PE curriculum

- actively promoting 'Walk to School Weeks'

- walking buses

- active and positive play in the playground

- links to the School Sport Coordinator Programme

- 'wake and shake' clubs

- high-quality out of school hours learning (OSHL)

- sports days

- regular inter-school competitions

- regular intra-school competitions

- non-competitive sports festivals

- attractive notice boards giving clear messages

- regular rewards assemblies

- links to local clubs and other agencies

- participation in the *Active Every Day* programme.

Combined with the above, schools should actively promote a campaign of healthy eating and drinking. Consultation with school meal providers and the recent publicity surrounding Jamie Oliver's initiative have brought the issue of improving school meals firmly onto the political agenda. As a result, there has never been a better time to re-educate both parents and children as to the benefits and value of proper nutrition. Schools can actively promote healthy eating and drinking in the following ways:

- healthy snacks for breaktime

- fizzy drinks off the menu

- healthy food and drinks in vending machines

- 'design a healthy menu' competition

- water fountains around the school

- individual water bottles for each pupil

- pupils allowed to drink water as they need it

- parental workshops and discussion groups.

Safety considerations

Each activity in this manual includes appropriate safety tips, but there are also some general issues that teachers must be aware of when undertaking physical activity.

Limited space activities

If activities are to be performed in the classroom, makes sure that the children have sufficient room to swing their arms or legs without injuring themselves or others. Check that there is nothing on the floor that could be tripped over or anything protruding that could be bumped into.

Hall activities

Ensure that the floor is free from debris including food, mud or litter. Keep the activity away from free-standing equipment such as pianos or music stands.

Outside/playground activities

Check the surface to be used to ensure that there is no broken glass, loose gravel or anything children could slip on and hurt themselves. Ensure that any activity you are doing is well away from any boundary walls or fences. Some of the activities involve children running at quite high speeds; these should be avoided if the area is wet or slippery.

Clothing and footwear

Children do not have to change in to PE kit for these activities as this would eat in to the allocated 10 minutes, but correct footwear must be worn. Pupils should wear training shoes for outside work and trainers/pumps or bare feet for the activities in the hall or classroom, depending on the nature of the activity.

Jewellery

Children should not wear jewellery while performing the activities as it can injure both themselves and other children.

Water

Children should have access to drinking water and be allowed to drink when necessary. During a 10-minute activity session it is unlikely that children will need to drink, but at the conclusion of the session water should be freely available.

Not immediately after eating

It would not be sensible to use the *Active Every Day* programme directly after eating lunch as there is plenty of running and jumping included. Since the programme should ideally be used as a response to the needs of children and a break from their structured timetable, a session at this time is unlikely to be warranted.

High-impact activities

Care must be taken with some of the 'Skipping' and 'Stamina, speed and agility' activities as they can be strenuous and potentially dangerous for young children's growing bones, muscles and joints. Some might be considered to be relatively high-impact activities, so rest time should always be built into the allocated 10 minutes.

Warming up, Cooling down, mobilising and stretching

One of the major benefits of the *Active Every Day* programme is that the children do not need to perform a traditional warm-up, as most of the activities are in fact warm-ups in themselves. However, if you feel the need to add in a warm-up or cool-down activity as well as some mobilising and stretching activities, here are some suggestions and general principles.

Warming up

A warm-up should always start slowly and build up speed gradually. The teacher can lead this activity with the children starting off standing on the spot. The children can then begin by moving various parts of their bodies, including the fingers, toes, legs and arms. The head and trunk can also be included. Children can then include actions that move them from the spot, for example walking, jogging, skipping and so on.

Ideas for warm-ups

1. Ask the children to walk in and out of each other without bumping. When you blow a whistle or clap your hands, the children have to bend their knees and touch the floor. Continue using a slow jog, then running.
2. As above, but when you call out 'Stop!' the children have to stop still, showing good body control.
3. Ask the children to play 'follow the leader' in pairs. The front child can travel around the space any way they choose, for example walking, hopping or jumping, and their partner has to follow them.
4. Ask the children to use their walking to draw big letters on the floor, for example S, C or A. They can then jump, hop, skip or run the pattern. You can ask the children to write their own names in large letters on the floor.

Cooling down

A cool-down at the end of an activity session allows children to slow down and recover, ensuring they are ready to return to their normal class. Activities can be the reverse of the warm-up, culminating in the children performing slow movements in a stationary position.

Ideas for cool-downs

1. 'Sleeping lions': ask the children to lie on the floor and stay as still and quiet as they can. Walk among them and, if they are still and quiet, tap them on the foot. This is their cue to get up quietly and line up ready to go back to class.

2. Ask the children to stand in a space and stretch up tall, then relax down to the ground and curl up small.

3. Ask the children to hold hands and make a large circle, and join the circle yourself. Walk round, keeping in the circle, but gradually get slower and slower until you come to a complete stop.

4. Ask the children to hold hands with a partner and walk around the area slowly. They should gradually slow down and curl up small on the floor.

Mobilising joints

These exercises help to loosen the joints and make them ready for exercise. They need to be performed slowly and with control. Children can perform 5–10 of each exercise, but must ensure they repeat the exercise on each side of the body (that is with both legs/arms).

Waist twists

Purpose
To loosen and warm up your waist and middle.

How to perform
Face the front with your knees slightly bent. Keep your feet facing the front and twist the top half of your body around to one side, then repeat on the opposite side. Your arms should be up level with your shoulders with your elbows bent and palms facing down.

Side bends

Purpose
To loosen and warm up your lower back and sides.

How to perform
Stand straight with your feet shoulder-width apart and your hands on your hips. Bend to the side without tilting forwards or back. Your knees should be slightly bent at all times.

Shoulder rolls

Purpose

To loosen and warm up your shoulders.

How to perform

Make sure you are in a space. Keep your arms slightly bent and move them in a circular motion, both backwards and forwards. Make sure you move them in both directions on both sides of the body.

Knee-lifts

Purpose

To loosen and warm up your knee and hip joints.

How to perform

Stand facing the front. Lift one knee up, keeping the rest of your body upright. Perform a clap under your lifted knee. Repeat with the other knee.

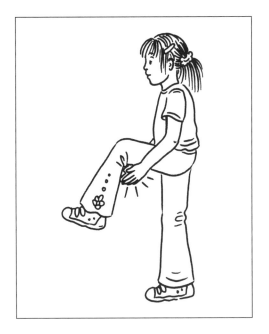

Static stretches

You can select three or four stretches appropriate to the activity and include them during a warm-up or as part of a cool-down. The stretches should be performed slowly and with control, and held for a count of 6–10 seconds. Remember to stretch both sides of the body. Make sure you breathe when stretching.

Whole-body stretch (standing)

Purpose
To stretch all your major muscles.

How to perform
Stand up straight, facing the front. Reach up tall with both hands, as far as possible. Keep your feet flat on the floor to avoid overbalancing.

Whole-body stretch (lying)

Purpose
To stretch all your major muscles.

How to perform
Lie down on your back (on a mat if possible). Stretch your arms above your head – they should be touching your ears – and point your toes.

Active Every Day: Key Stage 1 © Linda Kelly and Wendy Seward 2006, A & C Black Publishers Ltd

Quads (front of upper leg) stretch

Purpose
To stretch the muscles in the front of your upper leg.

How to perform
Lie down on your front (on a mat if possible). Reach behind you and hold your ankle. Push your hip in to the floor.

Groin stretch

Purpose
To stretch the muscles in your groin area.

How to perform
Sit on the floor with your head and upper body straight. Bend your knees and press your feet together. Push gently down on the inside of your legs with your elbows.

Hamstring (back of upper leg) stretch

Purpose
To stretch your hamstring (back of upper leg) muscles.

How to perform
Stand straight and put one leg out in front of you. Keep that leg straight and take your weight on to the back leg. Slightly bend the back/supporting leg. Tilt your bottom slightly forwards.

Calf (back of lower leg) stretch

Purpose
To stretch your calf (back of lower leg) muscles.

How to perform
Stand facing the front with both feet facing forwards. Keep your back leg straight with your heels on the floor. Bend your front leg and lean forwards slightly.

Active Every Day: Key Stage 1 © Linda Kelly and Wendy Seward 2006, A & C Black Publishers Ltd

Chest stretch

Purpose
To stretch the muscles across your chest.

How to perform
Stand up straight. Put your hands at the base of your spine, facing downwards. Squeeze your elbows together.

Triceps (bottom of upper arm) stretch

Purpose
To stretch your triceps (bottom of upper arm) muscles.

How to perform
Stand facing the front. Take one hand and place it over your shoulder, reaching down to the centre of your back. Use your other hand to keep the elbow high.

Dynamic stretching

These dynamic stretching exercises are fantastic as they stretch and mobilise the muscles and joints in one exercise. They should be performed steadily and with control.

Walking high knee-lift

Purpose
To work on buttock flexibility and hip and shoulder mobility.

How to perform
Walk slowly forwards, bringing your knee up to create right angles at your knee and hips. At the same time, bring up the opposite arm to create right angles at the elbow and shoulder.

Walking lunges

Purpose
To stretch the front of the hip and thigh.

How to perform
Walk slowly and, as you step forwards, bend your knees so your back knee touches the floor. Your back heel will come off the floor. Ensure that you keep the top half of your body upright.

Heel flicks

Purpose
To stretch the front and back of your thighs.

How to perform
Jog forwards, flicking your heels up to touch your bottom. Put your hands behind your back on your bottom with the palms facing out. To be done correctly, each flick must touch your hands.

Walking hamstring stretches

Purpose
To stretch your hamstring (back of the thigh) muscles.

How to perform
Walk slowly to a count of four and, on every fourth step, straighten your front leg and sink down on to your back leg. This leg should bend, and you can push down on to it with your hands. The toes of your front leg should be pointing up.

Walking single knee-lifts

Purpose

To work on buttock flexibility and hip mobility.

How to perform

Walk slowly to a count of three, bringing your knee up to create a right angle at your knee and hip on every third step. After doing 10 lifts to one leg, repeat on the other leg.

Who am I?

- Choose one child and ask him or her to decide on the name of a sports personality and whisper the name to you, then take a seat at the front of the class (the 'hot seat').

- Tell the rest of the class that they are allowed to ask eight questions to help them guess the personality.

- The child at the front of the class can only answer yes or no to each of the questions.

- If the class guesses the celebrity after eight questions, choose another child to take the hot seat and start the game again.

- If not, the child in the hot seat reveals who the celebrity was, then chooses another celebrity and the challenge begins again.

- You will need to discuss strategies with the children to make sure the questions are not random. Discuss what sort of questions would narrow the possibilities: for example, 'Are you male?' would give a clear answer, whereas 'Are you male or female?' would waste one of the chances as it wouldn't provide a yes or no answer.

Suggested space Classroom

Learning outcomes To identify a personality using questioning techniques.

Resources None

Health and safety Remind children about being sensitive to their peers.

Simplification Let the child in the hot seat use mime, like in charades, to help them give the rest of the class clues.

Extension Allow fewer questions, for example five.

Limited space

Clap and Repeat

- Ask the children to get into pairs and number the children in each pair one or two.

- Number one starts by clapping once.

- Number two copies the action.

- Number one then claps twice.

- Number two copies the action.

- Once the children are familiar with the idea of copying, ask number one to make the clapping sequence more complicated. Number two has to try to follow.

- After a few minutes, tell the number ones that they can now include a stamp of the feet or a nod of the head.

- Again, the number twos try to follow the sequence, including the new elements.

- After a few minutes, ask the children to swap so that number two is the leader of the sequence and number one the follower.

- Discuss with the children what made the sequences easier or more complicated.

Suggested space Classroom

Learning outcomes To follow a sequence with accuracy and develop your own sequences to be copied.

Resources None

Health and safety Ensure the children have enough space in which to work.

Simplification Use clapping only, without any other actions.

Extension Give the sequence a specific requirement, for example 'It must include a clapping sequence, two nods, a turn and a stamp'.

Fish 'n' Chips

- Ask the children to sit at their tables, close their eyes and rest their head on their arms.

- At random, choose a child by gently touching his/her arm.

- That child should then raise his/her head and, in a disguised voice, say 'fish 'n' chips'.

- Once they have heard that child speak, the rest of the class can raise their heads.

- The objective of the game is for the children to try to identify who said 'fish 'n' chips'.

- Use questioning techniques to discover what strategies the children used to identify the voice, for example, 'How did you know it came from that direction?' and 'How did you know if it was a girl or a boy?' You may need to help the children guess by asking questions such as 'What direction did it come from?' and 'Was it a boy or a girl?'

Suggested space Classroom

Learning outcomes To react to a voice in a particular part of the room and identify it.

Resources None

Health and safety Remind the children of the need for sensitivity.

Simplification Work in table groups of approximately six.

Extension Use a clean handkerchief, held over the mouth, to muffle the sound.

Limited space

fish 'n' chips

Hear the Noise!

- Place the tambourine on your desk or on a table at the front of the classroom.

- Ask the children to sit at their desks with their eyes closed and listen carefully.

- Select one child by touching him/her on the arm. S/he has to walk up to the tambourine, pick it up as quietly as possible and walk back to his/her seat.

- If the other children hear the tambourine make a noise, they raise their hand.

- If 10 or more children raise their hands, the turn is over and another child is chosen to have a turn.

Suggested space Classroom

Learning outcomes To use care and control to move an object; to listen and identify a particular sound.

Resources A tambourine

Health and safety Make sure there is a clear pathway for the children to walk in.

Simplification Ask the children to just pick up and put down the tambourine.

Extension If just one child hears a noise, that turn is over.

Heads Down, Thumbs Up

- Ask the children to sit at their tables with their heads down, eyes closed and thumbs facing upwards.

- Choose four children to start at the front of the class. Each of them has to wiggle the thumbs of one of the children who is sitting down, then return to the front of the class. Note: it is important that each of the four only wiggles the thumbs of one child.

- Next, say 'Stand up if your thumbs have been wiggled'; four children should stand up.

- Those four children now have to try to guess which of the children at the front wiggled their thumbs.

- If they are correct, they swap places with the child they identified; if they are incorrect, they remain seated.

- Once any swaps have been made, restart the game.

Suggested space Classroom

Learning outcomes To react to a signal and try to guess who gave it.

Resources None

Health and safety Remind the children to take extra care when wiggling other children's thumbs.

Limited space

Parts of the Body

● Work with the children on one line of the verse at a time until they have learned it for themselves.

● As you speak each line, perform the appropriate action.

Touch your fingers,
Touch your toes,
Touch your ears,
And touch your nose.
Touch your head,
And touch your knee,
Touch your cheeks,
Count 1, 2, 3.
Touch your elbow,
Touch your chin,
Touch your tummy,
Do a spin.
Touch the floor,
Reach for the sky,
Face your partner,
Wave goodbye!

● Repeat as required.

Suggested space Classroom

Learning outcomes To identify different parts of the body.

Resources None

Health and safety Ensure that the children have enough room to turn around on the spot and touch the floor.

Extension Ask the children to move around while repeating the rhyme and performing the actions.

Pass the Squeeze

- Ask the children to sit down around their tables and hold hands.

- One of the children starts by gently squeezing the hand of the person next to him/her.

- On feeling the squeeze, the receiving child then squeezes the hand of the next person.

- The receiving child can reverse the squeeze by sending it back to the child who sent it to him/her.

- Repeat the activity several times, with the children crossing their hands in front of them so that they receive the squeeze in a different way.

Suggested space Classroom

Learning outcomes To react to a signal and act upon it.

Resources None

Health and safety Remind the children not to squeeze each other's hands too tightly.

Adaptation Instead of holding hands and squeezing, the children could place their hands palm down on the table and react to the table being lightly hit.

Limited space

Ship Ahoy!

- Ask the children to stand in a space, making sure they have enough room to swing their arms and march on the spot.

- Show the children the actions to accompany each command.

- Then call out the commands at random and ask the children to perform the appropriate action. Use as many or as few actions as you want, depending on the ability of the class.

- The commands and actions include:

'Climb the rigging'	climbing action on the spot using arms and legs
'Captain on deck'	stand up straight and salute
'Scrub the deck'	large scrubbing actions as if holding a broom
'Shark attack'	rapid swimming actions (breaststroke or front crawl)
'Man the wheel'	holding and turning an imaginary steering wheel
'Stormy weather'	sway from side to side

Suggested space Classroom or corridor

Learning outcomes To follow and repeat simple actions; to select and respond to appropriate actions.

Resources None

Health and safety Make sure the children are not too close to anyone else if they are swinging their arms.

Simplification Perform the actions yourself and ask the children to copy you.

Extension Ask the children to work in pairs and call out actions for their partner to perform.

Stuck on You

- Ask the children to walk steadily around the playing area, taking care to avoid each other and the furniture.

- When you call 'Change!' they have to change direction and continue walking steadily around the area. Repeat several times.

- Next, throw the die and call out the body part highlighted, for example 'Elbows'.

- The children have to turn to the nearest child and join together using the highlighted body part, for example elbows to elbows.

- Repeat the activity several times.

- Suggested body parts:
    - hands
    - toes
    - hips
    - elbows
    - knees
    - shoulders.

Suggested space Classroom or corridor

Learning outcomes To be able to identify various parts of the body; to work cooperatively with others.

Resources One large die with parts of the body clearly indicated; one large numbered die (for extension).

Health and safety Ensure the pairs of children are in a space when they try to join body parts.

Simplification Demonstrate how to join the body parts.

Extension Throw the numbered die as well as the body parts die and call out the number and the body part. The children have to make groups of that number and join together using that body part.

Limited space

The keeper of the keys

● Ask all of the children to sit on the floor and form a large circle.

● Choose one of the children to sit on a chair in the centre of the circle. Blindfold that child and give him/her a rolled-up newspaper to hold. Place the keys under the chair.

● Tell the story of a troll who is the keeper of the keys that unlock the magic kingdom. Only a very brave and clever person is able to steal the keys from under the chair of the troll.

● Choose one of the children to try to enter the circle and steal the keys without the troll hearing him/her.

● If the troll hears a sound, s/he can point to the source of the noise using the rolled-up newspaper. If the newspaper touches the intruder, s/he has to return to the starting place and another person is chosen to try to steal the keys.

● If the intruder manages to steal the keys, s/he becomes the troll and the game restarts.

Suggested space Classroom (if there is enough space for the children to form a circle)

Learning outcomes To use care and control to move an object; to listen and identify a particular sound.

Resources A bunch of keys; a rolled-up newspaper; blindfold for the child in the centre of the circle.

Health and safety Make sure there is a clear pathway for the children to walk in. Ensure the children are careful when aiming with the newspaper.

Adaptation Allow the children to make low noises to put off the keeper of the keys.

Bean Bag Control

- Give each child a bean bag and ask them to stand in a space.

- Ask them to pass the bean bag around their waists, changing hands when they need to.

- Then ask them to try the same thing with different parts of the body, for example legs, head, knees and so on.

- Next, ask them to repeat this while moving around the area at the same time.

- Then ask the children to stop and find a partner.

- In pairs, they explore different ways of passing the bean bag to their partner, for example over the head, between the legs, by twisting the waist and so on.

- Give the children targets to beat, for example six passes through the legs or 10 passes overhead.

Suggested space Hall or outside space

Learning outcomes To identify various parts of the body; to develop and practise the skills needed to control an object.

Resources One bean bag per child

Health and safety Ensure that the children have enough room, especially when they are bending down.

Adaptation Use different equipment, for example balls or quoits.

Control, coordination and accuracy

Animal Walk

● Ask the children to find a space in the hall.

● Talk about visiting the zoo and the different animals you see when you are there.

● Introduce one animal at a time, describing and showing how they move:

● Monkey	on hands and feet with bottom in the air
● Crab	on hands and feet with tummy facing up; ask the children to try to walk sideways in this position
● Rabbit	crouch down, place hands on the floor and jump feet to meet the hands
● Bear	on hands and feet, moving the same arm and leg to walk
● Caterpillar	on hands and feet in press-up position; walk feet towards hands and then walk hands away from feet
● Crocodile	shuffle on forearms and feet, with body close to the floor.

Suggested space Hall

Learning outcomes To work on controlling the body in a number of different positions; to coordinate different parts of the body.

Resources None

Health and safety Ensure that the floor is clean and dry before starting this activity.

Simplification Only use a couple of different animals.

Extension Ask the children to work in pairs with one performing the action and the other trying to guess the animal.

Can You Catch It?

- Give each child a bean bag and ask them to practise throwing it up in the air and catching it while standing still.

- Ask them, 'How many catches can you do before you drop the bean bag?'

- 'Can you clap before catching the bean bag?'

- 'Can you clap under your leg before catching the bean bag?'

- 'Can you turn around before catching the bean bag?'

- Now, ask the children to walk around, still throwing the bean bag up in the air and catching it.

- Ask them to count how many catches they can make while walking around.

- Make sure the children have their hands out in front of them in a good catching position.

- Ask the children, 'How can you help yourself to catch the bean bag?'

Suggested space Hall or outside space

Learning outcomes To examine the skill of catching; to practise the skill of catching to gain consistency.

Resources One bean bag per child

Health and safety Make sure the children look where they are going when they are walking around and catching.

Simplification Ask the children to do the exercises only while standing still.

Extension Use a ball instead of a bean bag, which will make the catching much more unpredictable.

Control, coordination and accuracy

In the Hoop

- Give each child a bean bag and ask them to get into pairs.

- Give each pair a hoop.

- Ask each pair to put their hoop in a space and stand about 1 metre back from it.

- The children take it in turns to throw their bean bag, aiming to land them in the hoop.

- If they are successful, they can take a step back and throw from there.

- If they are not successful, they have to try again from that distance.

- The children carry on throwing and see how far away from their hoop they can get.

- Ask the children, 'What can you do to help you get the bean bag in the hoop?'

Suggested space Hall or dry outside area

Learning outcomes To practise throwing with accuracy; to look at the principles of accurate throwing.

Resources One hoop per pair; one bean bag per person.

Health and safety Make sure there is enough room so that groups do not have to throw across the path of other groups.

Adaptation Position the hoop against a wall or fence, either on the ground or with one child holding it.

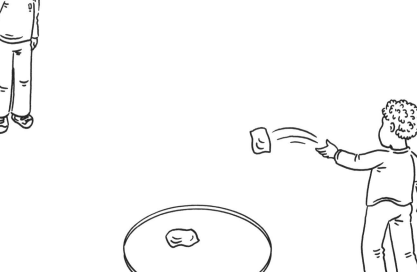

Balance the Bag

- Give each child a bean bag and ask them to stand in a space.

- Ask them to try to balance the bean bag on different parts of their body. These could include:

  - Palms of hands

  - Backs of hands

  - A thigh (by lifting up the leg)

  - Top of the arm

  - The head

  - Knees (by lying down)

  - Foot (with leg raised)

- Ask the children if they can move around, keeping the bean bag balanced on any of these body parts.

Suggested space Hall or outside space

Learning outcomes To identify certain parts of the body; to develop and practise the skills needed to balance an object.

Resources One bean bag per child

Health and safety Ensure there is plenty of room, especially when the children are bending or lying down.

Adaptation Use different equipment, for example quoits.

Control, coordination and accuracy

Hoop Ball

- Ask the children to get into pairs and give each pair a hoop and a medium-sized ball.

- Ask them to find a space, put the hoop on the floor and stand one to each side of the hoop.

- The first child bounces the ball in to the hoop and the other child attempts to catch it.

- That child repeats the exercise by bouncing the ball in the hoop for the first child to catch.

- Next, ask each pair to join up with another pair and put one hoop and one ball away.

- Two children stand to each side of the hoop.

- The pairs take it in turns to bounce the ball in the hoop. If the other pair does not catch the ball, the pair doing the bouncing get the point.

- The winners are the first pair to reach five points.

Suggested space Hall or dry outside space

Learning outcomes To practise bouncing a ball accurately; to work cooperatively with a partner.

Resources One hoop and one medium-sized ball per pair

Health and safety Ensure there is plenty of room.

Adaptation Instead of asking the children to bounce the ball in a hoop, ask them to bounce the ball over a line.

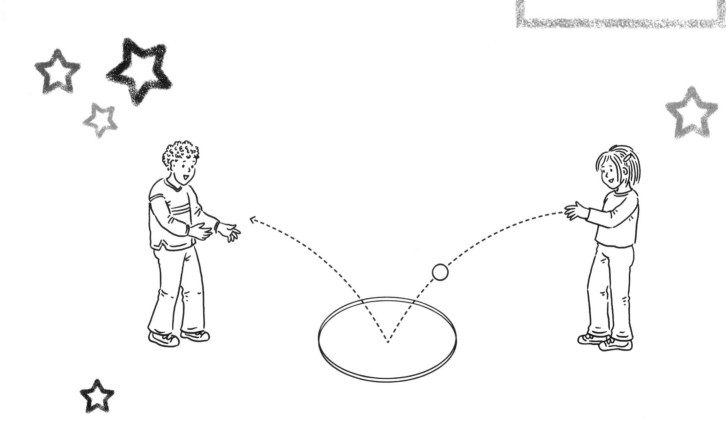

Grandmother's Foosteps

- Stand at one end of the wall and ask all of the children to stand at the other end of the hall, facing you.

- Turn around and face the wall so your back is to the children.

- The children then start creeping towards you.

- After a few seconds, turn around. If any of the children are moving, send them back to the start – the children have to be as still as statues when you turn around.

- The winners are the children who reach you (or the end of the hall) first.

- The game takes good body control to move and then stay suddenly still. Ask the children, 'How do you stop yourselves wobbling?'

Suggested space Hall

Learning outcomes To practise using body control to achieve stillness; to examine how we use our muscles to stay still.

Resources None

Health and safety Ensure the children are moving slowly and with control.

Adaptation Instead of walking, ask the children to crawl towards you.

Control, coordination and accuracy

Find the Space

- Ask the children to get into pairs and stand one behind the other in a space.

- Give the first child a sequencing spot to use as a steering wheel.

- Ask the children to move around the designated space like cars, avoiding all the other 'road users'.

- Call out traffic light colours and other commands for the children to follow, for example:

Red	Stop
Amber	Slow down
Green	Go
Change driver	Swap the person in front

- The children have to follow your instructions.

Suggested space Hall or outside space

Learning outcomes To explore basic skills, actions and ideas; to work cooperatively in a shared space.

Resources One sequencing spot (coloured round rubber mat) per pair

Health and safety Make sure the children are aware of all the other children around them. Remind them to keep their heads up when running to avoid collisions.

Simplification Put the children in to mixed ability pairs.

Extension Hold up a sheet of coloured paper rather than saying the words, so the children have to watch you carefully to follow the instruction.

Hoop Release

- Put the children into teams of five or six; the teams then play against each other.

- Mark out a playing area approximately the size of one third of a netball court. Divide the space in half using a bench or markers and place a hoop at the back of each area (the 'release area').

- Ask each team to stand on one side of the playing area.

- The aim of the game is for the children to throw the balls and try to hit their opponents below the hips. A hit above this area does not count.

- If a player is hit, he/she has to sit out.

- If a child throws the ball at the hoop and manages to bounce it in the hoop, any of his/her team's players who are out can re-enter the game.

- The winning team is the one who gets all of their opponents out.

Suggested space Hall or dry outside space

Learning outcomes To practise the skills needed to throw a ball with accuracy; to work cooperatively within a team.

Resources Two large soft balls for each group of five children; two hoops for each group of 10 children; bench or markers to divide the playing area.

Health and safety Ensure there is plenty of room for this activity.

Adaptation Include more than one hoop/release area.

Control, coordination and accuracy

Catch it if You Can

- Divide the children into groups of approximately 10.

- Ask nine of the children to form a circle, with the tenth child standing in the centre holding the ball.

- On your signal, the child in the centre should throw the ball to each child in turn for them to catch.

- If anyone drops the ball, they have to go down on one knee and stay there until the ball is thrown back to them.

- If they catch it the second time, they can stand back up.

- If they drop it again, they have to go down on both knees.

- The last person standing becomes the thrower for the next game.

- If everyone is able to catch well, you can either change the shape or size of the ball (for example a rugby ball or tennis ball) or widen the circle.

Suggested space Hall or dry outside space

Learning outcomes To practise throwing and catching a ball accurately; to work cooperatively within a team.

Resources One large ball per group of 10.

Health and safety Ensure that there is plenty of room for this activity.

Adaptation Change the shape or size of the ball. Introduce another thrower into the centre of the circle so two balls (perhaps of different sizes) are moving around together.

Follow the Leader

- Ask the children to get into pairs and number themselves one and two.

- Number one stands in front, with number two standing behind him/her.

- Number one starts by walking around the playing area with number two following. Child number one can take any pathway he/she wants: zigzag, curved, spiral and so on.

- Call out different ways of travelling for the children to try, for example jumping, skipping, hopping and so on.

- Every few minutes, swap the children over so number two gets a chance to be the leader.

- You can also suggest changes in level as the children travel, for example up high on tiptoes, crouched down and so on.

Suggested space Hall or outside space

Learning outcomes To explore different ways of travelling; to observe and copy different ways of moving.

Resources None

Health and safety Remind the children to look where they are going so they don't bump into other children.

Adaptation The children can perform the activity in groups of three or four. Make sure they all have a turn at being the leader.

Teamwork and cooperation

Mixed Pairs

- Tell the children that the idea of this game is for them to pair up with someone who has something in common with them.

- Ask the children to start moving around the playing area.

- Call out, 'Children, make a mixed pair of . . .'

- Ideas for the mixed pairs include:

  - Both with the same hair colour.

  - Both with the same eye colour.

  - Both with the same colour shoes.

  - Both with the same colour jumper.

  - Both live in the same street.

  - Both sit at the same table in class.

  - Both the same sex.

  - Both have a pet.

  - Both have a brother.

  - Both have a sister.

- Any children who are able to make a pair get a point. The child with the most points at the end of the game is the winner.

Suggested space Hall or outside space

Learning outcomes To communicate with the other members of the class; to work together cooperatively to fulfil a task.

Resources None

Health and safety Make sure the children don't grab the person they want to make a pair with – ask them to hold hands instead.

Adaptation Instead of looking for similarities, ask for pairs with differences, for example one girl and one boy, different hair/eye colour and so on.

Know the Name

- Ask the children to get into groups of no more than 10 and form a large circle.

- Give a ball to one child in each group. S/he has to roll the ball across the circle to another child and, as they do so, call out his/her own name.

- The game continues with the children rolling the ball across the circle and calling out their own name. This gives all the children a chance to learn the names of everyone in the class.

- The children cannot roll the ball to the child next to them.

- After a few minutes, change the game so the children have to call out the name of the person they are rolling the ball to.

Suggested space Hall or outside space

Learning outcomes To get to know the other children in the class; to work cooperatively with a large group.

Resources One large ball per group of 10.

Health and safety Make sure the children bend their legs when they bend down to roll the ball.

Simplification Use much smaller groups with only five or six children per group.

Extension Ask the children to throw the ball rather than rolling it.

Teamwork and cooperation

Duck, Duck, Goose

- Ask the children to sit on the floor in a large circle.

- Select one child to walk around the outside of the circle tapping each child on the shoulder, saying 'duck' as they tap.

- S/he picks one child and, instead of saying 'duck', says 'goose'. This child then gets up and chases the tapper around the outside of the circle.

- It is then a race to see who can get back to the empty place first. Whoever gets there first sits back down and the other person is the tapper for the next round of the game.

- Repeat the game, ensuring that as many children as possible have a go at being the 'goose' and the 'tapper'.

Suggested space Hall

Learning outcomes To practise responding quickly to a command; to work cooperatively and safely within a group situation.

Resources None

Health and safety Ensure that there is enough room for the children to run safely around the circle.

Adaptation The children can perform this activity in smaller groups of six to eight. This will ensure that they all have a turn. Make sure there is enough room for the children to run around each circle.

Active Every Day: Key Stage 1 © Linda Kelly and Wendy Seward 2006, A & C Black Publishers Ltd

Find the Number

- Tell the children that the idea of this game is to join with other children in the class to make groups of the number that you call out.

- Ask the children to start moving around the playing area.

- Call out 'Children, make groups of . . .' (two, three, four, five and so on).

- There might be the odd time when the class does not divide equally into the number you call out, but try not to do this too often as it tends to be the same children who are left out each time.

Suggested space Hall or outside space

Learning outcomes To communicate with the other members in the class; to work together cooperatively to fulfil a task.

Resources None

Health and safety Ensure the children don't grab the person they want to make a pair with – ask them to hold hands instead.

Adaptation As well as asking the children to get in to groups of a specific number, ask them to do a task – for example, groups of four sitting down or groups of three jumping on the spot.

Circle Ball

● Ask all of the children to stand in a large circle and pass a large ball around the circle from child to child.

● When you say 'Change', the children have to pass the ball around the circle in the opposite direction.

● When the children have got quite good at this activity, add a second and third ball.

● With older children, ask them to stand a little further apart and throw the ball around the circle instead of passing it.

Suggested space Hall or outside space

Learning outcomes To work cooperatively in a large group; to listen carefully to commands and follow the commands accordingly.

Resources A large ball (size 5)

Health and safety Ensure that the children are watching the ball(s) at all times.

Adaptation Instead of having one large group, divide the children in to groups of approximately eight to perform the activity. Give one of the children the role of saying 'Change'.

Active Every Day: Key Stage 1 © Linda Kelly and Wendy Seward 2006, A & C Black Publishers Ltd

centipede

- If there are more than twenty children in the class, divide them into two groups.

- Ask the children to make a line or 'centipede'.

- The child at the front of the centipede is the leader and everybody else has to follow his/her method of travelling. This could be bunny jumping, hopping, sidestepping, up and down and so on.

- The centipede must stay together. You can ask the children, 'What do you have to do to make sure the centipede stays together?'

- You can also ask, 'How do you know when to change the way of travelling?'

- Change the leader often.

Suggested space Hall or outside space

Learning outcomes To work together cooperatively as a team; to examine ways of working together to keep the line together.

Resources None

Health and safety Ensure that the leader does not perform any of the activities too quickly for the other children to follow.

Simplification Divide the children in to much smaller groups.

Teamwork and cooperation

Catch and Duck

- Ask the children to get into groups of five or six and give each group a ball.

- Ask each group to make a circle with one child in the middle holding the ball.

- The child in the middle has to pass the ball to each of the other children in turn. The children in the circle pass the ball back to the middle child and then duck or crouch down to show they have had a turn.

- When all of the children except the middle one are crouched down, the middle child holds up the ball and the game is over.

- Change the middle child over after each round so they all get a turn in the middle.

- Suggest to the children that they get their hands into position, ready to catch the ball.

Suggested space Hall or dry outside space

Learning outcomes To work together cooperatively to complete the task; to practise the skills of throwing and catching.

Resources One medium-sized ball per group of five or six children.

Health and safety Ensure that there is enough room for all of the groups to work safely.

Simplification Ask the children to roll the ball instead of throwing it. You could also use a larger ball.

Extension Add a competitive element by asking the groups to race against each other to see who can complete the task the quickest.

The Train Game

- Ask the children to get into pairs and stand one behind the other, making a 'train'.

- Give each pair two cones and ask them to place them on the floor and stand between them – this is their station.

- The pairs then move around the playing area with the front child leading and the other child following.

- When you call out, 'Return to station!' each pair has to go back to their station.

- You can ask the trains to move at different speeds, from slowly up to fast.

- You can also call out, 'Return to nearest station!' and the pairs have to go to the nearest station.

- If you call out 'Lose a carriage!' when the children are in a station, the back child has to stay at the station when the front child moves away.

- You can then call out 'Return to station!' and the front child can then reclaim his/her carriage.

- If you call 'All change!' the children change front and rear positions.

Suggested space Hall

Learning outcomes To work cooperatively with others in a shared space; to follow your partner to perform simple movements.

Resources Coloured marker cones

Health and safety Ensure that the children have enough room to move around safely.

Simplification Ask the children to work on their own; each child will have their own 'station'.

Extension Ask the children to work in groups of three or four so the train is longer.

Teamwork and cooperation

Collect the Treasure

- Place one hoop in the centre of the playing area and put all the bean bags ('treasure') in it.

- Place the other four hoops in each of the four corners of the area (away from the sides or walls), each an equal distance from the central hoop.

- Divide the class into four equal groups and ask each team to stand by one of the corner hoops. This is their base.

- On your command of 'Go!' one member from each team runs out to the centre hoop, collects a bean bag then runs back and puts it in their base hoop.

- Repeat this with one child from each team running in turn until all of the bean bags have gone from the centre hoop.

- Stop the game at any time and count up the bean bags in each hoop to find the winning team.

- You can repeat the game with the children hopping or skipping to the centre hoop and running back.

Suggested space Hall or outside space

Learning outcomes To work together as a team to achieve a result; to work out a strategy for completing the task.

Resources Five hoops; about 30 bean bags.

Health and safety Ensure that only one child from each team is running at a time.

Simplification Stop the game when all of the bean bags have gone from the middle hoop.

Extension Ask the children to transport the bean bag on their head; if they drop it, they have to return it to the centre hoop.

Active Every Day: Key Stage 1 © Linda Kelly and Wendy Seward 2006, A & C Black Publishers Ltd

Beans

- Ask the children to find a space.

- Introduce and demonstrate the actions listed below one at a time.

- When the children are familiar with the commands and actions, call out the names of the beans at random; the children have to perform the appropriate action.

- The actions include:

  - Runner bean — the children run around the area

  - Jumping bean — the children jump up and down

  - Broad bean — the children make a large shape and stand still

  - String bean — the children make a tall, thin shape and stand still

  - Jelly bean — the children wobble about like jelly on a plate

  - Beans on toast — the children lie still on the floor

  - French bean — the children put one hand on their hip and twirl around, saying 'Ooh la la'

- Ask the children, 'Which of the actions made you laugh?'

- Ask the children, 'Which of the actions made you breathe faster?'

Stamina, speed and agility

Colours

- Ask the children to space out in the playing area, which should be a square or rectangular shape.

- Explain that each of the lines that make up the square or rectangular shape is a different colour – red, blue, yellow and green.

- When you call out a colour, the children have to walk to the appropriate line.

- Repeat several times, alternating the colours.

- Ask the children to walk with one hand on their tummy and one on their chest, then ask them, 'What is your breathing like when you are walking?'

- Next, change the game by calling out a certain way of travelling as well as the colour, so the children have to respond to two commands. For example, 'Red: running,' 'Blue: hopping,' 'Green: skipping,' 'Red: galloping,' 'Yellow: hopscotch,' and so on.

- Now ask the children to put one hand on their tummy and one on their chest, then ask them, 'What is your breathing like now, after you have done some faster exercise?'

Suggested space Hall or outside dry space

Learning outcomes To respond correctly to instructions; to examine the changes in breathing when exercising.

Resources None

Health and safety Ensure the playing area is large enough so the children are not jostling for space on the line.

Simplification Put down coloured markers on the lines so the children can see which line is which. Only call out colours and keep the way of travelling the same for each one.

Adaptation Instead of using lines, the children could travel to the corners of the room/space.

Cat and Mouse

- This is a game of tag.

- Use the cones to mark out a playing area no larger than 10m x 10m.

- Give all the children except for about four a coloured band, which they tuck in to the back of their trousers or skirt to give them 'tails' – these children are the mice.

- The four children without the bands are the cats.

- The cats have to chase the mice around the area and try to grab their tails.

- If a mouse has his/her tail removed, s/he is out and has to stand on the edge of the area.

- When all the mice have been caught, select four different children to be the cats for the next game.

- Ask the children, 'Has your breathing got faster?' and 'Have you got any hotter?'

Suggested space Hall or dry outside space

Learning outcomes To control the body when moving at speed; to explore activities that make you breathe faster.

Resources One coloured band per child; four cones to mark out the playing area.

Health and safety Ensure that the playing area is dry as this activity includes quick movements with changes of direction.

Stamina, speed and agility

Fill the Box

● Put the box in the middle of the playing area and scatter all of the objects around the hall.

● Explain to the children that the idea of the game is to pick up the objects one at a time and place them back in the box. If they get all of the objects in the box, they win. You will be standing by the box and throwing the objects back out.

● Slow down the throwing out towards the end, so that the box actually gets filled up and the children win.

Suggested space Hall

Learning outcomes To work on speed and agility; to work cooperatively and safely in a space with other children.

Resources A box and lots of small equipment such as bean bags, quoits and so on – you need more than one object per child.

Health and safety Ensure that the children don't push each other to get to pieces of equipment.

Simplification Throw the objects back out of the box slowly.

Extension Use four boxes, one in each quarter of the room; the children can only put a specific colour or type of equipment in each box.

Active Every Day: Key Stage 1 © Linda Kelly and Wendy Seward 2006, A & C Black Publishers Ltd

Statue Tag

- Use the four cones to mark off the playing area, which should be about the size of a netball court.

- Tell the children that this is a game of tag. Give four of the children coloured bands to wear – this identifies them as the catchers.

- The catchers have to chase the other children around the area and try to tag them.

- If a child is caught, s/he has to stand still like a statue with his/her arms outstretched.

- When all of the children have been caught and are standing still, the game is over. Choose four different children to be the catchers and restart the game.

- Ask the children, 'Has your breathing got faster?' and 'Have you got any hotter?'

Suggested space Hall or dry outside space

Learning outcomes To control the body when moving at speed; to explore movements that make you breathe quickly.

Resources Four coloured bands; four cones to mark out the playing area.

Health and safety Ensure the playing area is dry, as this activity includes quick movements and changes of direction.

Adaptation Tell the children that they can release children from their statues by running under their arms. This will prolong the game.

Rabbit Holes

- Give each child a hoop. If there aren't enough to go around, ask the children to get in to pairs and give each pair a hoop.

- Ask the children to place their hoops on the floor in a space.

- The children have to move around the area in a variety of ways, avoiding the hoops. They can move by walking, running, skipping, hopping, bunny hopping, walking tall and so on.

- When you call out 'Down the hole!' the children have to jump in to a hoop and stay still.

- As a variation, you can call out a colour before you call 'Down the hole!' The children then have to find a hoop of that colour to jump in to (several children can fit in to one hoop).

Suggested space Hall

Learning outcomes To experience a variety of different ways of travelling; to follow instructions.

Resources One hoop per child (if possible)

Health and safety Tell the children to be careful not to step on the hoops when they are travelling around as they might slip.

Adaptation Instead of calling out 'Down the hole!' you can be a 'fox'. Walk around the area and whenever you get close to a child, s/he has to jump in to a hoop and stay still.

Over and Under

- Ask the children to get into groups of six and stand one behind the other in a line, with a small space between each child. The child at the front of the line should be standing at a marker cone.

- Each member of the group should stand comfortably with their legs apart as the ball needs to travel through their legs.

- Give the child at the front of each line a ball. On your signal, s/he passes the ball back between their legs to the next child.

- That child collects the ball and passes it through their legs to the next child. This continues until the child at the back of the line has the ball.

- S/he then runs to the front of the line, holding the ball, and stands at the marker. The rest of the group will need to shuffle back so that the child with the ball can start at the marker.

- The children then repeat the action until the original child is back at the front of the line.

Suggested space Hall or playground

Learning outcomes To increase levels of speed, agility and awareness; to roll a ball accurately.

Resources A large ball (size 4 netball or similar); one cone per group of six children.

Health and safety Ensure that there is enough space between the children so they don't bump their heads when bending forwards.

Adaptation The ball can be passed through the legs of one child and then over the head of the next child, continuing the pattern down the line.

Stamina, speed and agility

Snowballs

- Use the marker cones to divide the playing area in half.

- Give each child a ball and divide the group in to two equal teams. Ask each team to start on one side of the area.

- On your command, the children have to throw their ball over to the other side of the hall (like throwing a snowball).

- They then pick up one of the balls that has been thrown to their side and quickly throw it back. The children must be standing still when they throw the ball.

- The game is very quick, so the children need to react very quickly to pick up and throw back the ball.

- After about two minutes, stop the game and count up the balls on each side. The winning team is the one with the fewest balls on their side.

- Repeat the activity, stopping after another two minutes to see which team has won this time.

Suggested space Hall

Learning outcomes To move quickly around a small area with good body control; to work together cooperatively as a team.

Resources One sponge tennis ball per child; marker cones.

Health and safety Ensure that the balls are sponge so that they won't hurt the children when they are hit.

Number Challenge

- Ask all of the children to sit down cross-legged in a large circle.

- Place the bean bag in the centre of the circle.

- Give the children numbers from one to six around the circle.

- When you call out a number, for example 'four', all the children with that number have to get up and run clockwise around the circle.

- When they get back to their place, they go through the gap and try to be the first person to pick up the bean bag.

- Whoever picks up the bean bag replaces it and calls out the next number (but not their own).

Suggested space Hall or outside space

Learning outcomes To remember and follow a command; to work safely and cooperatively with the rest of the class; to increase levels of fitness and awareness.

Resources One bean bag

Health and safety Make sure the children stay on their feet when attempting to pick up the bean bag. Tell the children not to overtake other children when running around the circle.

Simplification The children can run only as far as their original chair, without having to retrieve the bean bag.

Extension Give the children sums to do to work out which number should run, for example: '4 + 2 = ?' '10 − 8 = ?' '2 x 2 = ?' and so on.

Stamina, speed and agility

Shuttle Relay

- Split the class into teams of approximately four to six children. Set out two marker cones per team – one to show the start position, the other 5 metres away.

- Ask the children to line up in their teams behind their marker cone.

- Ask the children to jog in a relay formation (one after the other) around the furthest cone and then return to the starting point.

- This continues until all the children have had a go.

- Now, change the drill so the children have to skip to the cone and run back.

- The next drill could be hop to the cone and run back.

- Continue, using a mixture of jogging, hopping, jumping, sidestepping, hopscotch and so on.

- Ask the children, 'Which way of moving made you breathe the fastest?' and 'Why do you think that is?'

Suggested space Hall or outside space

Learning outcomes To examine the types of exercises that make you breathe harder; to follow a set of instructions to complete a task; to increase levels of fitness and awareness.

Resources Two marker cones per group of four to six children (you will need a third cone if you use the extension activity)

Health and safety Ensure there is enough room between groups.

Extension Introduce another cone and give the children an additional action to use to reach it.

Tiger in the Jungle

Ask the children to get into pairs and stand in a space. One of them is the tiger, the other is the prey.

Teach the children the rhyme a line at a time, showing them the appropriate actions.

Tiger in the jungle
Stalking his prey *(the child who is the tiger starts walking around the area slowly, watching his/her prey)*
One step, two step *(the tiger takes two steps forwards; the prey takes two steps back)*
Jump out of the way! *(the prey jumps out of the way and the tiger follows)*

Dodge to the left and weave to the right *(the prey dodges and weaves and the tiger follows)*
Duck down quickly, get out of sight! *(the prey ducks down and hides and the tiger looks for him/her)*
Wriggle on your belly, slowly to your knees *(the prey wriggles on his/her belly and rises slowly to his/her knees; the tiger moves around the room looking for him/her)*
Skip along quickly and hide in the trees! *(the prey skips to the edge of the room and makes a statue)*

Tiger in the jungle
Stalking his prey *(the child who is the tiger starts walking around the area slowly, watching his/her prey)*
One step, two step *(the tiger takes two steps forwards; the prey takes two steps back)*
Jump out of the way! *(the prey jumps out of the way and the tiger follows)*

Ahhh! Too late! *(the tiger captures the prey)*

Repeat as required.

Suggested space Classroom, corridor or hall, depending on space

Learning outcomes To relate movement and action to singing and verse; to remember a sequence of movements and actions.

Resources None

Health and safety Ensure that the children have enough room to perform the activity.

Action rhymes

Head, Shoulders, knees and Toes

🟤 Ask the children to find a space.

🟤 Teach them the rhyme a line at a time, showing them the actions as you go along.

Head, shoulders, knees and toes, knees and toes, *(touch each body part as you sing the song)*
Head, shoulders, knees and toes, knees and toes, *(touch each body part as you sing the song)*
And eyes and ears and mouth and nose, *(touch each body part as you sing the song)*
Head, shoulders, knees and toes, knees and toes. *(touch each body part as you sing the song)*

🟤 Repeat the verse without saying 'head', but still touch the body part.

🟤 Repeat the verse without saying 'head, shoulders', but still touch the body part.

🟤 Repeat the verse without saying 'head, shoulders, knees', but still touch the body part.

🟤 Repeat the verse without saying 'head, shoulders, knees and toes', but still touching the body parts.

🟤 Repeat the initial verse, saying all of the words and touching the body parts.

Suggested space Classroom

Learning outcomes To follow a sequence of actions that accompany a song.

Resources None

Health and safety Ensure the children have enough room to perform the actions.

Active Every Day: Key Stage 1 © Linda Kelly and Wendy Seward 2006, A & C Black Publishers Ltd

Here We Go Round the Mulberry Bush

● Ask the children to stand in a large circle, holding hands.

● The children gallop in a circle during the chorus of the song and perform the appropriate actions while standing still for the verses.

(chorus)

Here we go round the mulberry bush, the mulberry bush,
   the mulberry bush,
Here we go round the mulberry bush on a cold and frosty
   morning.

This is the way we brush our hair, brush our hair, brush our
   hair,
This is the way we brush our hair on a cold and frosty
   morning. *(the children pretend to brush their hair)*

(repeat chorus)

This is the way we clap our hands, clap our hands, clap our
   hands,
This is the way we clap our hands, on a cold and frosty
   morning. *(the children clap their hands)*

(repeat chorus)

This is the way we stamp our feet etc. *(the children stamp
   their feet)*
This is the way we clean our teeth etc. *(the
   children pretend to brush their teeth)*

Suggested space Hall

Learning outcomes To relate movement and action to singing and verse; to remember a sequence of movements and actions.

Resources None

Health and safety Ensure that there is enough space for the children to gallop safely in a circle.

Simplification Only use the first two verses and repeat them several times.

Extension Ask the children to think up their own verses and appropriate actions.

Action rhymes

In a Cottage in a Wood

- Ask the children to stand away from their desks in a space.
- Teach them the rhyme a line at a time, showing them the appropriate actions.

In a cottage in a wood, *(make a rectangular shape with hands in front of body)*
A little old man at the window stood, *(hand above eyes to show someone looking)*
Saw a rabbit running by, *(use index and middle fingers to demonstrate rabbit ears and move them from side to side)*
Knocking at the door. *(pretend to knock at a door)*
'Help me! Help me! Help me!' he said' *(as each 'help me' is said, raise hands in the air in mock horror)*
'Or the hunter will shoot me dead!' *(imitate the hunter shooting his gun)*
'Come little rabbit, come inside, *(beckon the rabbit inside)*
And happy we shall be!' *(demonstrate a happy, smiling face)*

Repeat as required.

Suggested space Classroom

Learning outcomes To relate movement and action to singing and verse; to remember a sequence of movements and actions.

Resources None

Health and safety Ensure that the children have enough room to perform the activity.

Jack in the Box

● Ask the children to stand away from their desks in a space.

● Teach them the rhyme a line at a time, showing them the appropriate actions.

Jack in the box is a funny old fellow, *(pull a funny face)*
His clothes are dark red and his hair is bright yellow, *(point to clothes and hair)*
Slowly he stirs from his place way down low, *(crouch down and begin to wake)*
He turns round and round and gets ready to go. *(turn and begin to rise slowly)*
The lid opens quickly and out springs old Jack, *(jump up with arms above head)*
He jumps for a moment 'til it's time to go back, *(jump on the spot a couple of times)*
Around and around as the lid's firmly shut, *(slowly go down, turning as you go)*
Jack's back in the box and has to stay put!

Until . . . (repeat the rhyme as required)

Suggested space Classroom

Learning outcomes To relate movement and action to singing and verse; to remember a sequence of movements and actions.

Resources None

Health and safety Ensure that the children have enough room to perform the activity, especially the jumping actions.

Action rhymes

Jelly on the Plate

- Ask the children to stand in a space.

- Teach them the rhyme a verse at a time, showing them the appropriate actions.

- 'Wibble wobble' can be a gentle, appropriate movement of the arms, legs or whole body, as space allows.

Jelly on the plate, jelly on the plate,
Wibble wobble, wibble wobble,
Jelly on the plate.

Jelly on the floor, jelly on the floor, *(the children lie on their back)*
Wibble wobble, wibble wobble,
Jelly on the floor.

Jelly straight and tall, jelly straight and tall, *(the children stand up straight and stretch high)*
Wibble wobble, wibble wobble,
Jelly straight and tall.

Jelly far and wide, jelly far and wide, *(the children make themselves as wide as they can, arms and legs outstretched)*
Wibble wobble, wibble wobble,
Jelly far and wide.

Jelly side to side, jelly side to side, *(the children sway to the left and to the right)*
Wibble wobble, wibble wobble,
Jelly side to side.

Jelly on the plate, jelly on the plate,
Wibble wobble, wibble wobble,
Jelly on the plate.

Suggested space Classroom, hall or corridor

Learning outcomes To relate movement and action to singing and verse; to remember a sequence of movements and actions.

Resources None

Health and safety Ensure that the children have enough room to perform the activity.

46

Miss Polly

Ask the children to stand away from their desks in a space.

Teach them the rhyme a line at a time, showing them the appropriate actions.

Miss Polly had a dolly who was sick, sick, sick, *(pretend to rock a doll from side to side)*
So she called for the doctor to come quick, quick, quick. *(pretend to be speaking on the telephone)*
The doctor came with his bag and his hat, *(indicate the doctor's bag and his hat)*
And he knocked on the door with a rat-a-tat-tat. *(pretend to knock on a door in time to the rhyme)*
He looked at the dolly and he shook his head, *(look carefully and shake your head)*
And he said, 'Miss Polly, put her straight to bed!' *(wag your finger)*
He reached in his pocket for a pill, pill, pill, *(reach in your pocket to find the pill)*
'I'll be back in the morning with my bill, bill, bill'. *(wave as you walk away)*

Repeat as required.

Action rhymes

Moon and Stars

- Ask the children to stand away from their desks in a space.

- Teach them the rhyme a line at a time, showing them the appropriate actions.

Reach for the moon and reach for the stars, *(stretch up high left and right)*
Imagine you're the first person walking on Mars, *(moonwalk on the spot)*
Skip across Jupiter, *(skip on the spot)*
Land on the Sun *(jump and land)*
Ouch, ouch, it's hot, so you'd better run! *(run on the spot)*

Jump in the sea and strike out for land, *(jump and then pretend to be swimming)*
There's somebody there, they're waving a hand, *(wave your hand)*
Lie on the beach, stretch out in the heat, *(stretch out wide)*
Wiggle your fingers and wiggle your feet, *(wiggle your fingers and feet)*
Jump up and down and count up to ten, *(jump up and down and count to ten)*
Now it's time to start over again!

Repeat as necessary.

Suggested space Classroom

Learning outcomes To relate movement and action to verse; to remember a sequence of movements and actions.

Resources None

Health and safety Ensure that the children have enough room to perform the activity.

My Bonnie Lies Over the Ocean

- Ask the children to stand away from their desks in a space.

- Teach them the rhyme a line at a time, showing them the appropriate actions.

My Bonnie lies over the ocean, *(indicate the ocean by gently rolling your right hand in front of you)*
My Bonnie lies over the sea, *(indicate the ocean by gently rolling your left hand in front of you)*
My Bonnie lies over the ocean, *(indicate the ocean by gently rolling your right hand in front of you)*
So bring back my Bonnie to me. *(beckon Bonnie back by calling with index finger)*

Bring back, bring back, *(link arms with the person next to you and gently swing each other around)*
Bring back my Bonnie to me, to me, *(change arms and gently swing each other around)*
Bring back, bring back, *(beckon Bonnie back by calling with index finger)*
Bring back my Bonnie to me.

Repeat as necessary.

Suggested space Classroom

Learning outcomes To use simple actions in conjunction with a rhyme.

Resources None

Health and safety Ensure that the children have enough room to carry out the activity.

Extension Ask the children to make up further verses and actions to go with them.

Action rhymes

Oranges and Lemons

- Choose two children and ask them to form an arch using their arms.

- Ask all of the other children to link hands and pass under the arch, singing the song as they do so.

> 'Oranges and lemons,' say the bells of St Clements,
> 'I owe you five farthings,' say the bells of St Martins,
> 'When will you pay me?' say the bells of Old Bailey,
> 'When I grow rich,' say the bells of Shoreditch,
> 'When will that be?' say the bells of Stepney,
> 'I do not know,' say the great bells of Bow.
> Here comes the candle to light you to bed,
> Here comes the chopper to chop off your head.

- As the children sing the last line, the children forming the arch drop their arms to trap two children.

- The trapped children now form a new arch and the rhyme is repeated.

Suggested space Classroom

Learning outcomes To learn a rhyme and perform actions to accompany it.

Resources None

Health and safety Remind the children to take care when linking hands and bringing the arms down to trap a pair of children.

The Farmer's in his Den

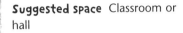

- Ask all of the children to form a circle.

- Choose one child to start in the centre of the circle as the farmer.

The farmer's in his den, the farmer's in his den,
Ee eye ee eye, the farmer's in his den.

The farmer wants a wife, the farmer wants a wife,
Ee eye ee eye, the farmer wants a wife.
(the farmer chooses a child to be the wife and join him in the centre of the circle)

The wife wants a child, the wife wants a child,
Ee eye ee eye, the wife wants a child.
(the wife chooses someone to be the child and join them in the centre of the circle)

The child wants a dog, the child wants a dog,
Ee eye ee eye, the child wants a dog.
(the child chooses someone to be the dog and join them in the centre of the circle)

The dog wants a bone, the dog wants a bone,
Ee eye ee eye, the dog wants a bone.
(the dog chooses someone to be the bone and join them in the centre of the circle)

We all pat the bone, we all pat the bone,
Ee eye ee eye, we all pat the bone.
(everyone lightly pats the child playing the part of the bone)

Repeat as required, choosing a different child to be the farmer.

Suggested space Classroom or hall

Learning outcomes To use actions to accompany a song.

Resources None

Health and safety Ensure that the children have enough room to perform the actions. Remind them to 'pat the bone' lightly.

Action rhymes

The Grand Old Duke of York

- Ask the children to stand away from their desks in a space.

- Teach them the rhyme a line at a time, showing them the appropriate actions.

The grand old Duke of York, *(move around in a very grand fashion)*
He had ten thousand men, *(indicate lots and lots of people using your fingers)*
He marched them up to the top of the hill, *(crouch down and gradually rise in a marching action)*
And he marched them down again. *(continue marching, going back down to a crouched position)*
And when they were up they were up, *(march and rise up)*
And when they were down they were down, *(march and crouch back down)*
And when they were only halfway up *(march and rise up to a position in between crouching and rising)*
They were neither up nor down.

Repeat as required.

Suggested space Classroom

Learning outcomes To match actions to a well-known rhyme.

Resources None

Health and safety Ensure that the children have enough room to perform the actions.

The Jockey

- Ask the children to stand away from their desks in a space.

- Teach them the rhyme a line at a time, showing them the appropriate actions.

- This rhyme can be spoken or sung as preferred.

The jockey sat on the horse, *(the children pretend they are on a horse, holding the reins and trotting on the spot)*
The horse could trot, of course, *(trot around the area)*
He set off at a pace, as if in a race, *(increase speed)*
And the jockey still sat on the horse. *(return to trot)*

The jockey sat on the horse, *(the children pretend they are on a horse, holding the reins and trotting on the spot)*
The horse could jump, of course, *(jump around the area)*
He jumped over the gate, as he was quite late, *(increase speed)*
And the jockey still sat on the horse. *(return to trot)*

The jockey sat on the horse, *(the children pretend they are on a horse, holding the reins and trotting on the spot)*
The horse could skip, of course, *(skip around the area)*
He skipped to the left and he skipped to the right, *(skip, changing direction)*
And the jockey still sat on the horse. *(return to trot)*

The jockey sat on the horse, *(the children pretend they are on a horse, holding the reins and trotting on the spot)*
The horse could canter, of course, *(run faster around the area)*
He cantered up high and he cantered down low, *(move up high and down low)*
And the jockey still sat on the horse. *(return to trot)*

Repeat as necessary.

Suggested space Hall or outside space

Learning outcomes To relate movement and action to singing and verse; to learn how to use space effectively.

Resources None

Health and safety Ensure that the children have enough room to perform the activity.

Action rhymes

This is the Way We Clap Our Hands

- Ask the children to stand away from their desks in a space.

- Teach them the rhyme a line at a time, performing the appropriate actions.

  This is the way we clap our hands, clap our hands, clap our hands, *(clap hands)*
  This is the way we clap our hands, on a cold and frosty morning.

  This is the way we stamp our feet, stamp our feet, stamp our feet, *(stamp feet)*
  This is the way we stamp our feet, on a cold and frosty morning.

  This is the way we stretch up tall, stretch up tall, stretch up tall, *(stretch up tall)*
  This is the way we stretch up tall, on a cold and frosty morning.

  This is the way we shake our hands, shake our hands, shake our hands, *(shake hands)*
  This is the way we shake our hands, on a cold and frosty morning.

  This is the way we slap our thighs, slap our thighs, slap our thighs, *(slap thighs)*
  This is the way we slap our thighs, on a cold and frosty morning.

  This is the way we nod our heads, nod our heads, nod our heads, *(nod head)*
  This is the way we nod our heads, on a cold and frosty morning.

  Repeat as required.

Suggested space Classroom

Learning outcomes To accompany a song with actions.

Resources None

Health and safety Ensure that the children have enough room to perform the actions.

Three Blind Mice

- Ask the children to work in groups of four. Give three of the children tags or bands to tuck in to the back of their trousers or skirt to make a 'tail' – these are the mice. The fourth child is the farmer's wife.

- Give each group a small area to work in, approximately ten feet by ten feet.

- The children sing the song to accompany the activity.

- At the beginning, the mice jog around the designated area.

- As the song develops, the farmer's wife tries to catch the mice and remove their tails.

Three blind mice, three blind mice,
See how they run, see how they run,
They all ran after the farmer's wife,
Who cut off their tails with a carving knife,
Did you ever see such a thing in your life,
As three blind mice?

Repeat with a new farmer's wife until all of the children have taken their turn.

Suggested space Hall or outside space

Learning outcomes To use space effectively, being aware of those around you.

Resources Tags or bands

Health and safety Ensure that the children have enough space to run around. Remind them to look up and be aware of those around them.

Learning How to Skip

- Ask the children to lie the skipping rope on the floor in a straight line.

- Ask them to perform the following actions:

  - Jump along the length of the rope from side to side.

  - Hop along the length of the rope from side to side.

  - Repeat, hopping on the other foot.

  - Without using the rope, jump up and down, including a bounce between each jump.

  - Tuck your elbows in and, using an imaginary rope, turn your hands from the wrists while at the same time performing the jump from the previous step.

- Next, ask the children to get into groups of three. Two children, one holding each end of the rope, rock the rope close to the floor. The third child has to jump the rope, including a bounce between each jump.

- Ensure that each member of the group has a turn at jumping the rope.

- Next, the children go back to using their own rope and practise jumping and turning the rope at the same time. Rest at regular intervals.

- Ask the children, 'How many skips can you do before the rope gets tangled? Can you beat your best score?'

- Remind them to rest between attempts.

Suggested space Hall or outside space

Learning outcomes To become familiar with a skipping rope.

Resources One skipping rope per child

Health and safety Ensure that the children have enough room to turn their rope without affecting the others. Ensure that the skipping ropes are the right size for the children.

56

Skipping Forwards

- Refer to 'Learning How to Skip' on page 56 for guidance.

- Remind the children of the jumping and bouncing action while turning the rope at the same time.

- Ask them to practise the skipping action.

- Next, show the children how to move from foot to foot (rather than jumping and landing on two feet) while turning the rope.

- Ask them to practise this for a few minutes.

- When they are ready, encourage the children to move around while turning the rope, so that they are skipping across the playground or hall area.

- Remind them to rest between attempts.

Suggested space Hall or outside space

Learning outcomes To learn how to skip effectively while turning the rope forwards.

Resources One skipping rope per child

Health and safety Ensure that the children have enough room to turn their rope without affecting the other children. Ensure that the skipping ropes are the correct size for the children.

Skipping

Skipping Backwards

- Refer to 'Learning How to Skip' on page 56 for guidance.

- Remind the children of the jumping and bouncing action while turning the rope at the same time.

- Ask the children to practise the skipping action.

- Next, encourage them to try turning the rope backwards while at the same time jumping the rope.

- Ask the children, 'How many jumps can you make before the rope gets tangled? Can you beat your best score?'

- Remind them to rest between attempts.

Suggested space Hall or outside space

Learning outcomes To learn how to skip effectively while turning the rope backwards.

Resources One skipping rope per child

Health and safety Ensure that the children have enough room to turn the rope without affecting the others. Ensure that the skipping ropes are the correct size for the children.

Skipping With a Partner

- Refer to 'Learning how to Skip' on page 56 for guidance.

- Remind the children of the jumping and bouncing action while turning the rope at the same time.

- Ask the children to practise the forwards skipping action, then the backwards skipping action.

- Next, ask them to get into pairs, put one of the skipping ropes away and put the other skipping rope to one side.

- Ask the pairs to practise jumping together with a bounce, without using the rope.

- When they can jump and bounce in time, ask them to try introducing the rope. One of the pair should turn the rope while both of them jump and bounce.

- When they can skip forwards, ask them to try turning the rope backwards.

- You could also ask the child who is not holding the rope to try turning around within the rope while jumping.

- Change the rope turner every few minutes.

- Ask the children, 'How many jumps can you make before the rope gets tangled? Can you beat your best score?'

- Remind them to take regular rests.

Suggested space Hall or outside space

Learning outcomes To learn how to skip effectively with a partner while turning the rope both forwards and backwards.

Resources One skipping rope per child

Health and safety Ensure that the children have enough room to turn the rope without affecting the other children. Ensure that the skipping ropes are the correct size for the children.

Skipping

Skipping with a Long Rope

- Refer to 'Learning how to Skip' on page 56 for guidance.
- Remind the children of the jumping and bouncing action while turning the rope at the same time.
- Ask them to practise the jumping action.
- Next, ask the children to get into groups of five. Show them how to turn a longer rope in pairs, ensuring that the turners keep the rope moving in time with each other.
- Ask them to practise turning the long ropes in pairs.
- Next, ask the children to stand in the rope one by one. The turners start turning the rope and each child jumps five times.
- Ensure that everyone, including the turners, has a go at this.
- Now, show the children how to time a jump in to a moving rope, continue jumping in the rope and time a jump out of a moving rope.
- Ask them to practise jumping in to a moving rope, performing five jumps and jumping out of a moving rope. Ensure that everyone, including the turners, has a go at this.
- Next, show children how to jump in to a moving rope one by one and continue to jump until all of the group have joined them in the rope.
- Once all of the children are jumping, they can then jump out of the rope in the order in which they entered.
- Ensure that everyone has a turn at entering and exiting the rope and turning the rope.
- Remind them to take regular rests.

Suggested space Hall or outside space

Learning outcomes To learn how to skip effectively using a long rope, both individually and as part of a larger group.

Resources One long skipping rope between every five children

Health and safety Ensure that the children have enough room to turn the rope without affecting the other children. Ensure that the skipping ropes are long enough for the number of children who will be jumping in them.

Adaptation Include a skipping rhyme to focus the children and extend their level of jumps.

Appendix: Checklists

In the appendix are a number of forms for use by both you and the children in your class. One of these is simply a record sheet to remind you which activities you have done, with room to record appropriate comments. The other three forms are for use by the children and could be used at any time of the year, either on their own or as part of a linked, cross-curricular project or themed week. These include:

1.   A questionnaire to give you an insight into individual children's opinions/attitudes towards physical activity.

2.   A daily physical activity record sheet, which looks at the amount and range of physical activities children participate in, both in and out of school. It also asks children to think about how exercise affects breathing patterns.

3.   A weekly physical activity record sheet, which looks at the amount and range of physical activities children participate in, both in and out of school. It also asks the children a range of questions relating to activity patterns.

Attitudes to physical activity

Name _____ Date _____

Colour in the face that fits how you feel about each sentence.

	Yes	Sometimes	No
1. I enjoy physical activity	🙂	😐	☹️
2. I like to play with others	🙂	😐	☹️
3. I find physical exercise easy	🙂	😐	☹️
4. I like running and jumping	🙂	😐	☹️
5. I find throwing and catching easy	🙂	😐	☹️
6. I like to learn new things	🙂	😐	☹️
7. I find it easy to remember rhymes and songs	🙂	😐	☹️
8. I play games with my friends	🙂	😐	☹️
9. I play games with my family	🙂	😐	☹️
10. I take part in physical activity every day	🙂	😐	☹️

Daily physical activity record sheet

Name _____

Monday   Tuesday   Wednesday   Thursday   Friday   Saturday   Sunday

(Circle the correct day)

When?	What did you do?	Time spent in minutes? *(colour in one block per minute)*										Did you enjoy it? *(colour in the face)*
Before school physical activity												☺ 😐 ☹
Break/lunch time												☺ 😐 ☹
Lesson time												☺ 😐 ☹
After school												☺ 😐 ☹

- What was your total time in minutes?_____

- Did you enjoy what you did? _____

Weekly physical activity record

Name _____ Date _____

Colour in the star if you took part in some physical exercise

Monday	☆ School lessons	☆ Lunch/break times	☆ After-school activity	☆ Evening activity
Tuesday	☆ School lessons	☆ Lunch/break times	☆ After-school activity	☆ Evening activity
Wednesday	☆ School lessons	☆ Lunch/break times	☆ After-school activity	☆ Evening activity
Thursday	☆ School lessons	☆ Lunch/break times	☆ After-school activity	☆ Evening activity
Friday	☆ School lessons	☆ Lunch/break times	☆ After-school activity	☆ Evening activity
Saturday	☆ Morning		☆ Afternoon	☆ Evening
Sunday	☆ Morning		☆ Afternoon	☆ Evening

● How many stars did you colour in? _____

Active Every Day: Key Stage 1 © Linda Kelly and Wendy Seward 2006, A & C Black Publishers Ltd

Activity checklist

Theme	Activity	When used	Comments
Limited space	Who am I?		
Limited space	Clap and Repeat		
Limited space	Fish 'n' Chips		
Limited space	Hear the Noise!		
Limited space	Heads Down, Thumbs Up		
Limited space	Parts of the Body		
Limited space	Pass the Squeeze		
Limited space	Ship Ahoy!		
Limited space	Stuck on You		
Limited space	The Keeper of the Keys		
Control, coordination and accuracy	Beanbag Control		
Control, coordination and accuracy	Animal Walk		
Control, coordination and accuracy	Can You Catch It?		
Control, coordination and accuracy	In the Hoop		
Control, coordination and accuracy	Balance the Bag		

Activity checklist

Theme	Activity	When used	Comments
Control, coordination and accuracy	Hoop Ball		
Control, coordination and accuracy	Grandmother's Footsteps		
Control, coordination and accuracy	Find the Space		
Control, coordination and accuracy	Hoop Release		
Control, coordination and accuracy	Catch It If You Can		
Teamwork and cooperation	Follow the Leader		
Teamwork and cooperation	Mixed Pairs		
Teamwork and cooperation	Know the Name		
Teamwork and cooperation	Duck, Duck, Goose		
Teamwork and cooperation	Find the Number		
Teamwork and cooperation	Circle Ball		
Teamwork and cooperation	Centipede		
Teamwork and cooperation	Catch and Duck		
Teamwork and cooperation	The Train Game		
Teamwork and cooperation	Collect the Treasure		

Active Every Day: Key Stage 1 © Linda Kelly and Wendy Seward 2006, A & C Black Publishers Ltd

Activity checklist

Theme	Activity	When used	Comments
Stamina, speed and agility	Beans		
Stamina, speed and agility	Colours		
Stamina, speed and agility	Cat and Mouse		
Stamina, speed and agility	Fill the Box		
Stamina, speed and agility	Statue Tag		
Stamina, speed and agility	Rabbit Holes		
Stamina, speed and agility	Over and Under		
Stamina, speed and agility	Snowballs		
Stamina, speed and agility	Number Challenge		
Stamina, speed and agility	Shuttle Relay		
Action rhymes	Tiger in the Jungle		
Action rhymes	Head, Shoulders, Knees and Toes		
Action rhymes	Here We Go Round The Mulberry Bush		
Action rhymes	In a Cottage in a Wood		
Action rhymes	Jack in the Box		

Activity checklist

Theme	Activity	When used	Comments
Action rhymes	Jelly on the Plate		
Action rhymes	Miss Polly		
Action rhymes	Moon and Stars		
Action rhymes	My Bonnie Lies Over the Ocean		
Action rhymes	Oranges and Lemons		
Action rhymes	The Farmer's in his Den		
Action rhymes	The Grand Old Duke of York		
Action rhymes	The Jockey		
Action rhymes	This is the Way we Clap our Hands		
Action rhymes	Three Blind Mice		
Skipping	Learning How to Skip		
Skipping	Skipping Forwards		
Skipping	Skipping Backwards		
Skipping	Skipping with a Partner		
Skipping	Skipping with a Long Rope		

Active Every Day: Key Stage 1 © Linda Kelly and Wendy Seward 2006, A & C Black Publishers Ltd

Bibliography

DfES and DCMS (2003), *PE, School Sport and Club Links Strategy (PESSCL)*

DoH (Spring 2004), *Choosing Health? Choosing Activity: a consultation on how to increase physical activity*

Scheuer, L. J. and Mitchell, D. (2003), *Does Physical Activity Influence Academic Performance?,* SportaPolis newsletter May 2003 (http://www.sports-media.org/sportapolisnewsletter19.htm)

Scottish Executive (2004), *Report of the Review Group on Physical Education*

Index